Black Nova Scotians

John N. Grant

Drawings by Azor Vienneau

Biographical Material courtesy Nova Scotia Human Rights Commission

Nova Scotia Museum
Halifax, N.S.
1980

Published by
The Nova Scotia Museum
as part of
The Education Resource Services Program
of the
Department of Education
Province of Nova Scotia

Hon. Terence R. B. Donahoe
Minister

Gerald J. McCarthy
Deputy Minister

Design by Nova Scotia Museum

Produced by
the Nova Scotia Communications and
Information Centre.

Printed in Canada

© John Grant 1980
ISBN 0-919680-20-8

Canadian Cataloguing in Publication Data
Grant, John N.
   Black Nova Scotians

"Biographical Material courtesy Nova Scotia
Human Rights Commission".
Bibliography: p.
ISBN 0-919680-20-8 (pbk.)

1. Blacks — Nova Scotia — Biography. 2. Blacks
— Nova Scotia — History.   3. Nova Scotia —
History.   I. Vienneau, Azor.   II. Nova Scotia
Human Rights Commission.   III. Nova Scotia
Museum.   IV. Title.

FC2350. N4G72   971.6'00496   C81-096001-X
F1040.N3G72

Foreword

This brief account of Black people in Nova Scotia sketches the story of the Black Loyalists, the Maroons, and the Refugees of the War of 1812. A quick glance is also taken at the decline of slavery and the role of religion and education in the Black community.

Black Nova Scotians do have a heritage. It is a heritage that contains events, attitudes and struggles unique to Blacks. It is also a heritage that reflects provincial and national events as well as relationships between countries and ideologies. This paper will portray people in their environment, facing shared hardships of economy and climate, while struggling to overcome the special problems of racial prejudice.

The history of Black Nova Scotians is really two histories: first, this is an important chapter in the history of Nova Scotia, and second, it is the history of a people.

Any work, no matter how short, owes it existence to many people. to the individuals and the institutions that have assisted me, I owe thanks. For Betty, Julia, Heather, and Andrew.

John N. Grant

Immigrations:
 Black Loyalists from New York to Shelburne and Halifax, 1783.
 Maroons, Jamaica to Halifax, 1796.
 Black Refugees, Delaware and Chesapeake to Halifax, 1813-1815.
 Black Refugees, Delaware and Chesapeake to Halifax, via Bermuda, 1813-1815.

Emigrations:
 Black Loyalists, Halifax to Sierra Leone, 1792.
 Maroons, Halifax to Sierra Leone, 1800.
 95 Black Refugees, Halifax to Trinidad, 1821.

Contents

Foreword	3
The Pre-Loyalist Period	6
The Loyalist Period	8
The Emigration of the Black Loyalists	10
Guysborough Settlement	14
The Maroons	15
The Decline of Slavery in Nova Scotia	18
The Emigration of the Chesapeake Blacks	21
Emigration to Trinidad	27
The Passing Years	28
And The People Said Amen'	32
Black Nova Scotians to 1901	36
A Part of the Life	38
George Dixon	39
Dr. William Harvey Goler	40
William Edward Hall, VC	41
B. A. Husbands	42
Sam Langford	43
Portia White	44
Dr. William A. White	45
Bibliography	46

The Pre-Loyalist Period

The pioneers who came to settle Nova Scotia were not all White; some of them were Black. Records of Blacks are found as early as 1606, when Matthew de Costa, who had been a slave of the Portuguese, was registered as living in Port Royal. In 1686, Monsieur de Meulles, the Intendant of New France, made a census of the Acadians. In it he lists among the settlers of Cape Sable the name 'La Liberté, le neigre', (Liberty, the Black). Ten years later, at least one Black, a captive of the Indians, was known to be living in the northern portion of Acadia which later became the Province of New Brunswick. Both of these Black men may formerly have been slaves. La Liberté's name may have symbolized a successful escape from slavery. The second man was apparently taken by the French to New Brunswick.

Slavery in Nova Scotia

There had been African slaves at French Louisbourg but whether there were any at the early English capital of Annapolis or at the fishing port of Canso is not clear. That there were slaves in Halifax and these other places later, there can be no question. Reports in 1750 listed fourteen free Black people in the capital city, and slaves were used in the construction of a vessel in Halifax Harbour in 1751 by John Gorham.

Slave sales were held in Halfiax. For example, in 1752 the *Halifax Gazette* carried an advertisement which read:

> Just imported, and to be sold by Joshua Mauger, at Major Lockman's store in Halifax, several negro slaves as follows: a woman aged thirty-five, two boys aged twelve and thirteen respectively, two of eighteen and a man aged thirty.

This same Joshua Mauger, who was an important merchant in Halifax and later a member of Parliament in England, had slaves for crews on his sailing ships.

The newspapers also carried advertisements for runaway slaves and indentured servants. These advertisements often cautioned sea captains against taking escapees on board ship, which suggests one of the likely methods of escape.

All of the Blacks in Nova Scotia were not slaves; some were free and seem to have worked as servants in the household of the well-to-do. One Black woman servant, referred to as Sylvia, became the heroine of the American attack on Lunenburg during the American Revolution. She protected the children of her employer, saved some valuables from the raiders, carried powder and shot to the few defenders of the town and is said to have fired on the attackers herself.

During the pre-Loyalist period, there were very few Black people in the province. A census return made on January 1, 1767, gave the population of Nova Scotia as 13,374, and only one hundred and four of these persons were of African origin. Fifty-four of them were residents of Halifax, six lived at Annapolis, and the others were scattered about the province. The American Revolution and the subsequent immigration of the Loyalists provided the province with a large number of new citizens, both Black and White.

The Loyalist Period

During the American Revolution, the leader of the British forces, Sir Henry Clinton, offered freedom to any slaves who might flee their masters, cross to the British lines and fight for the British king. Many seized the opportunity and made their way, as did the White Loyalists, to New York, one of the last British strongholds. Others escaped and boarded the British ships or joined British raiding parties in the southern colonies.

The last real battle of the Revolutionary War was fought at Yorktown on October 19, 1781. There the French and Americans defeated the British forces. Two years later, the United States of America was formed. Many people who wished to remain under the rule of their king left the new republic. They were known as the Loyalists and about 50,000 of them came to the Maritime Provinces.

When the war was over, Sir Guy Carleton, over the objections of General George Washington and the American Congress, who claimed the Black Loyalists as property and sought their return to their 'masters', was determined to remove the Blacks from New York along with the other Loyalists under his charge. Included among the former slaves were the 'Black Pioneers', an all-Black regiment under the command of Colonel Bluck, described in the records of the time as a 'mulatto'. 'Pioneers' are comparable to engineers in today's armed forces. This was the only Afro-American regiment established by the British, although in many other regiments Black men served as buglers, labourers and teamsters.

Arrival of the 'Brigade of Blacks'

In July, 1783, Governor Parr of Nova Scotia noted that he was expecting a 'Brigade of Blacks' totalling 1,500 in number. They arrived at Shelburne in August and were, by order of the Governor, settled 'up the North West harbour'. They called their settlement Birchtown, likely after General Birch, the commandant of the city of New York. These

Blacks were promised not only free land but also, as was provided for all the immigrants, rations for three years and other aid necessary for their settlement. Other free Blacks were settled at Digby, Annapolis, Preston, and in Guysborough County. Some found employment in Halifax and the other larger centers. In total, it is estimated that 3,000 Black Loyalists came to Nova Scotia, of whom over one-half, 1,521, were mustered at Shelburne in 1784.

Together with the free persons of African origin, large numbers of slaves, also Black, were brought into Nova Scotia by their fleeing Loyalist 'masters'. A 'return of the disbanded troops and Loyalists settling in Nova Scotia' was made by Colonel Morse, commander of the Royal Engineers, in the autumn of 1783 and the summer of 1784 for the purpose of determining the number entitled to the 'Royal Bounty of Provisions'. In 1899, historian T. W. Smith commented on this return:

> In the column allotted to 'servants' are, Dartmouth, 41; Country Harbour, 41; Chedabucto, 61; Island St. John, now Prince Edward Island, 26; Antigonish, 18; Cumberland, etc., 21; Partridge Island, now Parrsboro, 69; Cornwallis and Horton, 38; Newport and Kennetcook, 22; Windsor, 21; Annapolis Royal, etc., 230; Digby, 152; St. Mary's Bay, 13; Shelburne ??; River St. John, 441; a total number, inclusive of some small figures not quoted, of twelve hundred and thirty-two persons, to nearly all of whom must have belonged the appellation of 'slave'.

As no slaves or 'servants for life' were recorded for either Shelburne or Cape Breton Island and as there is no doubt that they existed in both localities, the number 1,232 is not extravagant. It must be remembered, however, that some of those called servants were just that. During the period that the Loyalists were in New York, some of the Black ex-slaves were hired as servants by the well-to-do White Loyalists.

The Emigration of the Black Loyalists

As the 1780's wore into the 1790's, some of the heady enthusiasm and great expectations of the Loyalists disappeared. The planned role of the re-organized Maritime Provinces as suppliers of the West Indian market failed to be realized, as only the longest established settlements had foodstuffs available for export. Often faced with infertile and rocky land, and with isolation, and sometimes failing to make use of what opportunities were available, many initially flourishing White Loyalist communities dwindled to the point of disappearing.

The decline of these settlements and more especially of Shelburne, which threw many of Birchtown's bread-winners out of work, seriously affected the fortunes of hundreds of the Black Loyalists. Then in 1789 came a crop failure that resulted in a virtual famine. Faced with these setbacks and with racial intolerance and the militant opposition of White labourers, the Black settlers in Nova Scotia became disillusioned with what they had hoped would be a land of freedom. As the numbers of White Loyalists diminished, so too did the number of slaves in the province, since they were usually obliged to accompany their 'masters'. Many of the White Loyalists left 'Nova Scarcity', going to England or back to the United States. The Black Loyalists, however, could not return to the United States without risking a return to hated slavery.

A British military man described Birchtown as he and some companions saw it in November of 1790:

> After the review, Hood, Buller and myself walked through the woods about two miles from the barracks to a negro town called Birch Town. At the evacuation of New York, there were a great number of these poor devils given lands and settled here. The place is beyond description, wretched, situated on the coast in the middle of barren rocks, and partly sur-

rounded by a thick impregnable wood. Their huts miserable to guard against the inclemency of a Nova Scotia winter, and their existence almost depending on what they could lay up in summer. I think I never saw wretchedness and poverty so strongly perceptible in the garb and countenance of the human species as in these miserable outcasts. I cannot say I was sorry to quit so miserable a dwelling.

Faced with the life described above, it was no wonder that many of the Black settlers were disheartened and ready to attempt a fresh start.

Thomas Peters

Among the disillusioned free Black settlers of Nova Scotia was Thomas Peters, formerly a Sergeant in the regiment of 'Black Pioneers'. Peters had settled at Annapolis and later applied for land in New Brunswick. Upon the rejection of his application for land, Peters went to England, where he laid a petition of his grievances before Lord Grenville, Secretary of State for the Colonies. His petition stated specifically that he and other members of the 'Black Pioneers' did not receive the land that they were due. As a result of his efforts, in early August of 1791, dispatches on the subject of the treatment of the free Blacks were sent to Governors Parr of Nova Scotia and Carleton of New Brunswick. The Governors were reprimanded for the neglect complained of and ordered to inquire immediately into the facts, and, if the complaints were found true, they were to take the necessary steps to atone for the injustices.

A Commission was established to inquire into the matter. The Commission, whose report was not submitted until March 19, 1792, indicated that indeed many of the Blacks had not received their grants. But this, they reported, was due to the very large numbers who were calling upon the services of the Government's surveyors. Speaking of the Black settlers in general and Thomas Peters in particular, the Commissioners wrote; 'and . . . if he had not so hastily quitted it [the province], he would have received his full share of Provision and Land with [the] others.'

But the Black settlers had already waited several years and their patience was running thin; and no doubt the Black settlers, without capital or particular influence with the Halifax government, were often the last to be accomodated.

The Sierra Leone Company

The Governors had also been informed that Peters was interested in moving to a warmer climate and that the Sierra Leone Company had expressed an interest in the situation of the Blacks in Nova Scotia and New Brunswick. The Sierra Leone Company had been formed by a group of 'philanthropic' Englishmen who had shown concern for the plight of Africans in Great Britain. They expressed the hope, much of which was not eventually realized, to found a society in which Black men and White men would have equal status and equal opportunity for advancement. Accordingly, they had acquired a large area of land on the west coast of Africa which they called Sierra Leone.

At about this time, the Company was searching for potential settlers for their new country. With this in mind, the British Government had requested the Governors of Nova Scotia and New Brunswick to make inquiries as to how many of their free Blacks desired to emigrate to that African colony. Likewise, they were ordered to inquire as to the number of the Blacks who might be willing to enlist for service in the West Indies, either as a separate army corps or to be attached to a regiment on duty there. In their replies, the Governors insisted that no intentional injustice had been committed in their respective provinces, and that there was little interest in enlisting. On the other hand, how-

The uniform of a private in the 5th West India Regiment, c. 1815.

ever, a number of the Black persons were interested in emigrating to Sierra Leone.

On October 7, 1791, John Clarkson, an agent of the Sierra Leone Company, arrived in Halifax to take charge of the gathering and 'removing' of the interested Black Loyalists. Travelling widely throughout the province, Clarkson met with groups of Black settlers and explained the plan, arranged for lodging and transport, and saw to the details that necessarily accompany such an undertaking. Clarkson faced many diffuculties in his work. The first was the problem of travelling in Nova Scotia in those days. Then, too, he was not kept informed about the situation in England and in Sierra Leone. He was faced with White opposition to his plans. Many Whites had been told, although it was not true, that Clarkson planned to remove all the best and most industrious of the Black population and leave the rest to become charges on the government. Many also regretted seeing such a supply of cheap labour leave the country. By his exertions, Clarkson so completely expended himself physically that on the date of departure he had to be hoisted on board ship in a basket.

Efforts at Recruitment

It had also been part of the government's original intention to use Black dissatisfaction to benefit the British Empire by forming a West Indian regiment of Loyalist Blacks. To this end, a recruiting officer, Lieutenant Francis M. Miller, had come from the West Indies in early October. However, few were inclined to join the army rather than go to Africa.

Outward Bound

Early in the new year, with costs rising, enlistments for the new colony of Sierra Leone were cut off and transports were made ready for the voyage. On January 15, 1792, the fleet, consisting of 1,190 persons —222 of them from New Brunswick — left Halifax

Harbour bound for Africa. On board were groups from Shelburne, Digby, Preston, Halifax, Saint John, and other Black communities. The British government expended close to £16,000 on this emigration of the Black Loyalists — a large sum when it is considered that the entire budget of the Province of Nova Scotia in 1792 amounted to only £5,326.17.6.

On May 29, 1792, the *Royal Gazette* announced: 'We are happy to have it in our power to inform the public that the fleet which sailed from hence last January with the free Blacks, all arrived safe after a passage of forty days'. With this notice, the emigrated Black Loyalists disappear from Nova Scotia history.

Guysborough Settlement

One group of whom no record of emigration to Sierra Leone exists is the Black Loyalists of Guysborough County. They, some slave and some free, had arrived with the White settlers and the disbanded regiments which had received land in the Chedabucto Bay area. A Black community was developed behind the present-day village of Guysborough. One man, Thomas Brownspriggs, apparently was the leader of the Black community. Relatively well educated, he was respected in both the Black and White communities.

By early 1787 many of the Black settlers were becoming dissatisfied with their position. Led by Brownspriggs, they petitioned Lieutenant-Governor Parr for land for those who wished to become independent farmers. On September 28, 1787, Parr ordered Surveyor-General Charles Morris to 'lay out under Thomas Brownspriggs and seventy-three others at Tracadie . . . 3,000 acres.' One hundred and seventy-two Blacks had been expected to settle at Tracadie, but not all were willing to leave the Guysborough area, where some had found employment. In the new settlement, Brownspriggs and later Dempsey Jordan were the leading figures in both religious and secular matters.

The Maroons

The second immigration of free Blacks into the province, like the first, developed from events entirely divorced from Nova Scotia history. In Jamaica the Maroons had, from the time of the British conquest in 1655, waged war against the British colonizers of the island. After 140 years of intermittent warfare, the Jamaican Government succeeded in overcoming the Maroons in 1796. The Legislature, vengeful and certainly tired of the cost of maintaining order, decided to rid themselves of 'the problem'. Accordingly preparations were made for the removal of one group of Maroons, with plans for their settlement in Lower Canada (Quebec). Upper Canada (Ontario) had also been suggested as a suitable place, but it was finally decided that the group would be sent to Halifax and wait there until instructions were received from England. Two men, Messrs. Quarrell and Ochterloney, were sent from Jamaica with the Maroons as Commissioners.

On June 26, 1796, three transports, the *Dover, Mary* and *Anne* sailed from Port Royal Harbor, Jamaica. They arrived in Halifax, one on July 21 and the other two on July 23, landing 543 Maroon men, women and children. The Duke of Kent, then Commander-in-Chief of the British Army in North America, impressed with the proud bearing and other characteristics of the Maroons, employed the entire group to work on the new fortifications at Citadel Hill in Halifax. From them, the section of the Citadel known as 'the Maroon Bastion' received its name. When Lieutenant-Governor Sir John Wentworth suggested that the Maroons would be good settlers, he received instructions from the Duke of Portland to settle them in Nova Scotia 'if it could be done without injury to the colony'. Accordingly, the two commissioners responsible, with credit of £25,000 Jamaican currency from the government of Jamaica, expended £3,000 on 5,000 acres of land and construc-

tion in the neighborhood of Preston. Also, Governor Wentworth obtained an allowance of £240 annually from England for the support of a school and to provide religious instruction. Following the first winter, the Maroons, raised in an independent, dominating 'warrior' culture and not impressed with the apparently servile 'virtues' of cultivating the soil, became increasingly discontented. Wentworth wrote of them, 'They wish to be sent to India or somewhere in the east, to be landed with arms in some country with a climate like that they left, where they might take possession with a strong hand . . .'

The Maroons, reputed to be excellent fighters, were apparently organized shortly after they arrived into military units similar to the style of self-government they had used in Jamaica. In 1796, forty gross of coats with metal buttons, and sixty gross of vests, were ordered for their use. The insignia on the buttons was an alligator holding a wheat sheaf and an olive branch.

At this time the military authorities feared the French might attempt to recapture Nova Scotia by an invasion; and in 1797, Wentworth informed the British Government that he thought the Maroons would 'be useful and faithful corps to oppose an invading army'.

Emigration of the Maroons

The unusually severe winters of 1796-97 and 1797-98 increased the discomfort and shortened the tempers of the Maroons. In the spring of 1799, Sir John felt obliged to dispatch Captain Solomon and 50 men of the Royal Nova Scotia Regiment to Preston where they withheld supplies from the most refractory so as to maintain order. Wentworth meanwhile became increasingly disillusioned with the Maroons as settlers; besides, the money granted by the Jamaican government towards their support was running out. Since they would not accept the suggested ways of supporting themselves

The Maroons had had a semi-military political organization in Jamaica. Governor Wentworth maintained at least the semblance of this system and "appointed captains and majors among them. Officers' uniforms, ordered by Wentworth, included handsome coats and vests, cocked hats, scarlet cloth, and gold lace." The illustration above represents the design of the Maroon uniform buttons. The order to a London firm of button makers requested that they be of "strong white metal and showing an alligator holding within its mouth stems of ears of wheat and an olive branch with the words 'Jamaica to the Maroons 1796'."

and seemed likely therefore to become a charge on the public purse, the Lieutenant Governor, in accordance with their own demand, resolved that the best course of action would be to remove them.

In 1796, before the Maroons arrived in Nova Scotia, Sierra Leone had also been suggested as a possible place of settlement. The Sierra Leone Company however had refused to entertain the notion of receiving a 'body of Negroes whose reputation could not be held to warrant such a step'. The Company's objections were based on two reasons: first, because the earlier settlers from Nova Scotia were now in open rebellion against the Sierra Leone government; and, second, because the colony was said to be intended for Christian Negroes and many of the Maroons were not of Christian faith.

In 1799, the Secretary of State reopened negotaitions with the Sierra Leone Company on the subject of the Maroons. The Company remained unenthusiastic. Sir John Wentworth gave his approval to the scheme and added that the inhabitants of Nova Scotia would be pleased by removal of the Maroons. With the Sierra Leone Company finally persuaded to receive them, preparations were made for their transportation to Africa. 'On the 6th of August, [1800] Wentworth reported that they had embarked and were ready to sail.'

The second attempt at settling free Blacks in Nova Scotia had, like the first, ended with their eventual emigration. On October 1, 1800, the Maroons arrived in Freetown Harbor, Sierra Leone. When they disembarked, their assistance was requested by and given to, the Government of Sierra Leone to quell the insurrection of the Black Loyalists who had previously emigrated from Nova Scotia.

Although most of the Maroons seemed to have left Nova Scotia, some remained; for example, a census of the Black community at Tracadie in 1817 showed several persons to be of Jamaican ancestry.

The Decline of Slavery in Nova Scotia

Although the emigration of the Black Loyalists and the Maroons reduced the Black population of Nova Scotia, there remained in the province numbers of free Black settlers, located mainly in the urban centres. A number of Black slaves also remained.

In 1798, Jeremiah Northrup offered a reward through the **Royal Gazette** to any person who would bring to Mr. David Rudolph at Halifax, or to himself at Falmouth, a 'negro boy . . . a smart likely lad';

. . . and by certificates acknowledged before a justice of the peace James Cox of Shelburne in 1800 hired 'my slave, George Cox,' to Captain Samuel Mann, of the brig **Greyhound** for a coasting voyage to Newfoundland and back.

Slaves Sales
In 1804, a Black slave was sold in Annapolis and on March 2, 1807, Simon Fitch of Wolfville purchased a woman, Nelly, for £39 from the Allison estate in what is considered to be the last slave sale in Nova Scotia.

The latest known advertisement in Nova Scotia for a public sale of a Black slave appeared in the *Royal Gazette* and *Nova Scotia Advertiser* of September 7, 1790, in Halifax, while the notice of Daniel Brown in the New Brunswick *Royal Gazette* of October 16, 1809, is the last known advertisement for the private sale of a slave in this area. In the July 10, 1816 issue of the *Royal Gazette* of New Brunswick appears the last known offer of a reward for the apprehension of a runaway slave.

Anti-Slavery Feeling
These instances might serve to qualify the optimism of the statement made in October, 1796 by Governor Wentworth to the Duke of Portland that 'slavery being almost exterminated here, distinctions naturally painful to

these people (the Blacks) are gradually dying away.' This statement however may be illustrative of the spirit of the time. Anti-slavery sentiment in Nova Scotia followed public opinion at the time in England. The British government, pushed by various philanthropic individuals and groups, first declared it illegal to remove a slave from the country; then Judge Manfield's decision in 1772 declared 'the state of slavery so odious that nothing could support it but positive law,' and freed at least part of the nation's slaves. In 1807, the 'General Abolition Act' abolished the slave trade; and finally in 1833 slavery within the British Empire was abolished by Act of the Imperial Parliament.

In Nova Scotia, too, anti-slavery feeling was growing. The open letters and pamphlets of the Rev. James MacGregor, a Presbyterian minister, in 1788, damning the practice of slavery and those involved in it, received the sympathetic eye of most non-slaveholding Nova Scotians. In 1787 a clause inserted in an 'Act for Regulating Servants' was rejected by the House of Assembly on the grounds that slavery did not exist in the province, and ought not to be mentioned. Again, in April, 1789, a bill entitled 'The Regulation and Relief of the Free Negroes within the Province of Nova Scotia' was rejected by the Council, because passing it would mean recognizing the slavery of Blacks as a statute right.

The Case of James Singletory

The Courts, too, undermined the position of slave holders. In Shelburne, numbers of Black people sued their masters for freedom on the grounds that they were illegally held. The case of James Singletory is typical. On August 25, 1785, James Singletory applied to Magistrate James McEwan and asked to be freed from Samuel Anderson, formerly of St. Augustine, Florida. Anderson claimed Singletory, his wife, and his child as slaves, and one J. Fanning witnessed to the effect that he knew Singletory as the slave of Anderson in Florida. The Court, however, ordered Anderson to prove that Singletory was a slave by producing a bill of sale within twelve months or else to pay him wages. In the interval, Singletory was to be treated as a hired servant, not to be sold or removed from the province, and to be produced from time to time as the Court ordered. Further, both Anderson and Fanning were bound over to the Court, the former for £50, the latter for £25, which would be forfeited if the Court's ruling was disobeyed.

As most Loyalsits had been forced to move from their homes rather quickly, papers such as bills-of-sale were often lost and those unable to prove 'ownership' had to give up their slaves. On the other hand, in at least one recorded case, the master was able to prove 'ownership' and kept the slave.

'To Wear Out the Claim Gradually'

On other occasions, the Courts deemed it necessary to prove not only the immediate 'slave-holder's' right to hold or sell the slaves, but the 'right' of the person from whom they obtained the slaves to sell them. In Nova Scotia the Supreme Court, as well, placed obstructions in the path of the slave holder. Chief Justices Thomas Andrew Strange and his successor, Sampson Salter Blowers, both laboured on the bench for the slave, although neither seems to have made a direct ruling on the question of the legality of slavery. In a December 22, 1799 letter to Ward Chipman of New Brunswick, Blowers wrote:

> *My immediate predecessor dexteriously avoided any adjudication of the principal point, yet as he required the fullest proof of the master's claim in point of fact, it was found generally very easy to succeed in favour of the negro . . . a summary decision of the question of slavery between master and negro here has always been resisted, and the party claiming the slave*

has been put to his action; and several trials have been had in which the jury has decided against the master, which has so discouraged them that a limited service by Indenture has been generally substituted by mutual consent . . . I had frequent conversation with Mr. Strange on the question, and always found that he wished to wear out the claim gradually, than to throw so much property as it is called into the air at once.

In September, 1801, the case of James DeLancey vs. William Wooden was tried before the Supreme Court of Nova Scotia. It marked one of the last stages of the emancipation of slaves in the province. A slave, known only as 'Jack', escaped from DeLancey and, on arriving in Halifax, was employed by Wooden. DeLancey, hearing of this, demanded Jack's wages. In subsequent legal procedure, DeLancey's claim was upheld. However, Wooden's attorney, Richard J. Uniacke, requested the Courts to arrest judgment on the grounds that Jack and all others held as slaves in Nova Scotia were free. In 1803 the case was dismissed, and Jack retained his freedom.

The Disappearance of Slavery

In 1807 and 1808 the owners of slaves in Annapolis County made a last-ditch effort to preserve their 'property'. Hoping for relief by legislative action, they presented a petition to the House of Assembly. The petition, signed by 28 slave proprietors, complained that because of the Court's decisions they had no way to hold their slaves, who were leaving them daily. The petitioners requested either that 'such regulations that are required to bind their servants to them' be made or that they receive compensation for their losses. On the same date that the petition was presented, January 7, 1808, Mr. Thomas Ritchie, member for Annapolis, introduced a bill to 'regulate Negro servants within and throughout this province.' The bill provided for the gradual emancipation of the remaining Black slaves, with compensation from the public purse for the slave proprietors. Although given a second reading on January 11, 1808, the bill was deferred on the following day for three months, was never reconsidered and never became law.

As a result of the action of the courts and the rebuffed efforts to strengthen the system, the slaveholders' position was well described by one of their contemporaries: 'The masters hold them (the slaves) when they can but dare not bring the case to court.'

Following the action of the Legislature and the Courts the general opinion prevailed in Nova Scotia that slavery did not legally exist. In a country possessing neither the climate nor the fertility of soil to allow extensive plantation crops, any but domestic slaves were generally impractical. Coupled with slavery's unpopularity as a system was the uncertainty of being able to retain one's 'property'. As a result slavery slowly disappeared from the province.

Although slavery did exist in Nova Scotia at least into the first decade of the nineteenth century, it is likely that by the time of the arrival of the refugee Blacks of the War of 1812 slavery was largely a dead issue in the province. As no compensation was paid by the British Government to anyone in the Maritime Provinces for 'property' lost through passing of the British General Abolition Act of 1833, it is safe to assume that any person who could be classified as a slave after about 1815 was held by fear, force or personal choice rather than legal means. Tradition, however, tells of later instances of the illegal holding of people in slavery in some parts of Nova Scotia.

The Emigration of the Chesapeake Blacks

The War Background

During the first decade of the 1800's, England was still fighting Napoleon in Europe. Largely because of this war, and with both sides at fault, England's relations with the United States deteriorated. Finally on June 19, 1812, President Madison declared war against Great Britain. American forces invaded the Canadas (Ontario and Quebec) and were strongly opposed by a few British regulars and the Canadian militia, who were able to halt their advance. The land war ground to a stalemate. On the sea, the Americans won some spectacular victories in single-ship engagements, but the movement in force of the British Navy into the area gave the British the advantage in that field. Thereafter the British blockaded the sea coast, especially the areas of the Delaware and Chesapeake rivers, to prevent the Americans from trading with Europe.

To strengthen the war effort, the British sent Vice-Admiral Sir Alexander Inglis Cochrane to take command. Cochrane was a veteran of the Revolutionary War and wished to give the Americans 'a complete drubbing'. With his second-in-command, Sir George Cockburn, Cochrane landed raiding parties on the coast of the United States, strangled its commerce, harassed its population and finally burned its capital city of Washington. This was done in retaliation for the American burning of York (Toronto), the capital of Upper Canada.

The existence of a potential for a fifth column of Blacks within the ranks of the Americans did not go unnoticed by the British command. Admiral Warren, however, had been instructed not to incite rebellion among the Black slave population, although he was ordered to receive aboard his ships any Blacks who might ask him for assistance. These he was to receive as free men, not as slaves, and to send them to any of several of His Majesty's colonies. Captain Robert Barnie of H.M.S. *Dracon* reported to Admiral

Warren on the state of the Black population:

> The slaves continue to come off by every opportunity and I have now upwards of 120 men, women and children on board. I shall send about 50 of them to Bermuda in the Conflict . . . there is no doubt but the Blacks of Virginia and Maryland would cheerfully take up arms and join us against the Americans.

Warren relayed the information to the Admiralty, but no steps were taken to utilize it until Cochrane took command. On April 2, 1814, a proclamation was issued promising land and 'all due encouragement' to people who wished to leave the United States. Cochrane especially instructed his agents to tell the slaves that they would also receive their freedom if they crossed to British lines.

Hundreds of Blacks in the Chesapeake Bay states as well as in other areas of the British blockade seized their opportunity and made their way to the British vessels and the promised freedom. The British, knowing that the removal of slaves would reduce the affected area's contribution to the war effort, liberated several thousand. The British were also becoming increasingly opposed ideologically to institutionalized slavery, although they remained class conscious. The number of slaves freed included those who escaped on their own initiative, those who were encouraged by their fellows (sent back for that purpose) to escape, and those who had freedom forced upon them as a result of the continuous raids of the British marines. That most were completely willing to go is testified to by dispatches to the Governor of Virginia. In them, citizens complained of the numbers of escaping slaves, while the local military men claimed that the runaways were supplying the British with intelligence on American military activities.

Cochrane was determined to remove the slaves, not only to reduce the Americans' work force but also to recruit the ex-slaves as active soldiers and marines. In late April or early May, 1814, Cochrane ordered Cockburn to 'endeavor to raise a Corps of Colonial Marines, from the People of Color who escaped to us from the Enemy's shore in this neighboorhood [Chesapeake Bay] and to cause such as . . . may enlist for this purpose to be immediately formed, drilled and brought forward for service . . .' By May 9, a 'considerable number' had enlisted and an officer of the Royal Marines, William Hammond, was put in charge of their training; and later he commanded them in the field. Often mentioned in dispatches for their ability in combat, the Colonial Marines quickly proved a valuable addition to the British fighting force.

The presence of armed Blacks who 'conducted themselves with utmost order, forebearance and regularity [and who] were uniformly volunteers for the station where they might expect to meet their former masters' represented the worst fears of the southern slave-holders. On August 3, 1814, the Governor of Virginia received a petition, 'numerously signed', from the inhabitants of Caroline County against the call of the militia of that county into service elsewhere because of apprehension of Black insurrection. On the following day, it was reported to the American Adjutant General:

> Our negroes are flocking to the enemy from all quarters, which they convert into troops, vindictive and rapacious — with a minute knowledge of every by-path. They leave us as spies upon our strength, and they return upon us as guides and soldiers and incendiaries.

To them was attributed much of the effectiveness of British ambushes, as the Blacks knew the country so much better than did the officers of the American forces. In closing, the report expressed what must have been the fear of many of the inhabitants:

> The example . . . which is held out in these bands of armed negroes, and the weakness of the resistance which as yet has been made to oppose them, must have a strong effect upon those blacks which have not as yet been able to escape.

Without doubt the Black troops were producing the desired effect.

In September, 1814, Cochrane decided to combine the three hundred men of the Colonial Marines with two hundred from the Second Battalion of the Royal Marines to form a third battalion called the Royal and Colonial Marines. He was also determined to pay the Black troops an additional eight dollars bounty for their capable conduct. The Colonial Marines and the other refugees from the United States who had enlisted in different regiments, served throughout the remainder of the war until peace was signed on Christmas Eve, 1814, and in the anticlimactic battle of New Orleans.

The Arrival of the Chesapeake Blacks

Nearly 2,000 Black refugees came to Nova Scotia as a result of the War of 1812. Others went to Trinidad and elsewhere. For the freedom of the more than 3,000 slaves who escaped, the British authorities agreed to make a direct payment of £250,000, or $1,204,960, to the American Government. This was a prelude to the Act of 1833 which freed 800,000 slaves throughout the British Empire and allotted an expenditure of £20,000,000 for compensation.

More than half of the refugees who came to Nova Scotia arrived before 1815. The *Acadian Recorder* of September 18, 1813, made first announcement of the arrival of the former slaves. Thereafter, almost any Navy ship arriving in Halifax from the war zone to the south brought refugees. After their arrival, their names were recorded and the Oath of Allegiance was administered. Then they were permitted to seek employment. In the booming war economy of Nova Scotia, work was relatively easy to find, and the wages of 5 shillings to 7/6 (60 to 95 cents) per day were, for the time, high. There is no doubt that White workers and the more established Black Loyalists had a better chance of obtaining the good, more permanent jobs. But apparently the refugees who came to Nova Scotia during this final year of the war were able to get enough to at least support themselves.

The following year they were not so lucky. When the War 1812 came to an end, there was a general slowdown in the economy. The first to be phased out of their jobs were the refugees, and in the winter of 1815 it was reported they were 'in a deplorable state of distress and unable to earn their subsistence'. To make matters worse, an epidemic of smallpox broke out, obliging the Government to innoculate as many people as possible and to provide rations for the most destitute.

In the spring of 1815 the Provincial Assembly had met and discussed the situation of the refugees. They granted money to pay for the campaign against smallpox, but made it clear that they did not want any more Black immigrants to come to the province.

On April 1, 1815, in a 'humble address' to the Lieutenant-Governor the members of the House expressed 'concern and alarm at the frequent arrival in this Province of Bodies of Negroes and Mulattoes of whom many have already become burdensome to the Public.' The address pointed out that the House did not wish to expend public funds in the encouragement of settlers whose 'character, principles and habits are not previously ascertained,' and expressed the fear that the introduction of more of the immigrants could cause the 'Establishment of a separate and marked class of people unfitted by nature to this Climate or to an association with the rest of His Majesty's Colonists.' It concluded with the request that

> Your Excellency will use your endeavours to prohibit the bringing of any more of these people into this Colony, by making such representations to His Majesty's Ministers as Your Excellency may deem proper or taking such other Measures as to Your Excellency may seem expedient.

The wishes of the House of Assembly, however, were not to be gratified.

With the signing of the treaty of Ghent that ended the War of 1812, Vice-Admiral Cochrane had been faced with the problems of dismantling his war machine. Regular troops could be returned to Europe, where they were needed to deal with Napoleon, who had recently escaped from Elba Island, and was busy gathering another army. Colonial troops, raised for duty only in North America, had to be disbanded and provided for. The usual method was to provide incentives for their establishment as settlers in some part of the British possessions, often where they had enlisted. But in the case of the Colonial Marines this was not possible. At the close of hostilities, therefore, they were transported to Ireland Island, Bermuda, the site of the British naval base. There, as in Nova Scotia, hundreds of refugees who had not joined the forces had been sent. The Colonial Marines took over the jobs that had employed many of the civilian Black refugees. Ultimately the Colonial Marines were disbanded and they settled in Trinidad, where, paradoxically, they were invited to be the first line of defence in case of slave uprisings.

The establishment of the Colonial Marines at the Ireland Island Naval Base presented Cochrane with an additional problem —what to do with the dislocated refugee civilian workers who had lost their positions. As the local laws of Bermuda did not permit the settlement of free Blacks, he was forced to move them to a colony that would receive them. Thus, on March 25, 1815, he addressed a letter to Lieutenant Governor Sherbrooke of Nova Scotia informing him that he intended to send between 1500 to 2000 refugee Blacks from Ireland Island to Halifax.

Lieutenant Governor Sherbrooke received the letter on April 2. The British Government had earlier suggested that the Collector of Customs in Halifax be responsible for the 'Negro Department'. Sherbrooke had agreed to this plan and suggested that assistance should be given to those who would be willing to settle and cultivate land. He immediately placed the responsibility of caring for the expected Blacks in the hands of the Collector of Customs, T. N. Jeffery.

The Melville Island Depot

Jeffrey chose Melville Island, now the site of the Armdale Yacht Club, as the depot to which the refugees were to be taken for food, shelter, and medical care. This island had been used since the turn of the century as a compound for prisoners-of-war, and in 1808 a large wooden structure had been built to provide better accommodation for captives. On the outbreak of the War of 1812, American prisoners were added to the throngs of French inhabiting the island. The fall of Napoleon in 1814 and the news of peace with the United States, received early in 1815, fortunately emptied the prison of its occupants, leaving it available for the arrival of the Chesapeake Blacks. Without the protection offered by the island camp, it might have been necessary for the refugees to live in tents or in unsanitary, rat-infested hulks floating in the harbor. It was under such conditions that many of the Loyalists suffered during their first winter in Nova Scotia.

After the Treaty of Ghent ended the fighting in America, an additional 800 refugees arrived in Nova Scotia. Of these 727 came between April 27 and July 26, 1815. They were all received at Melville Island. A Halifax contractor was engaged to supply provisions to the refugees with a carefully stipulated diet, both for the healthy and for those in hospital.

In June, 1816, the Melville Island depot was closed. Sickness had taken a grim toll of the refugees, death carrying away as many as one-eighth of the 800 received at the island.

Plans for Settlement

Some of the 2,000 new Black citizens of Nova Scotia were able to obtain permanent employment, but the majority, unable to secure employment (as was the case with most immigrants) were provided with land. Perhaps mindful of the maxim 'out of sight, out of mind', the refugees requested land close to Halifax. Two areas, Preston and Hammonds Plains, were chosen as the sites of the major settlements. Other smaller settlements were established on the Cobequid Road, the Shubenacadie Road, the Windsor Road, Refugee Hill, Porter's Lake, Prospect Road, Fletchers Lake, Beaver Bank, Beech Hill and Dartmouth, and around the major settlements of Preston and Hammonds Plains.

Preston had been the location of two other Black settlements. Both the Black Loyalists and the Maroons were established in the area previously but without much success. The location was chosen again because there a large number of Blacks could be settled together and within easy reach of the Halifax market where the products of their labours could be sold. But the ten-acre lots granted to them were much too small. Both the Black and the White settlers of the area complained that no one could be expected to make a living on them. The fifteen-hundred-acre 'Commons' which was to supply 'fuel, fencing and building materials' for all the settlers was situated in such barren land that it was of very little use to anyone.

When the location of the settlements was agreed upon, an elaborate plan of development was formed. Fifty of the men were to be engaged to build log cabins before the winter set in. Sixteen were to work as sawyers to cut boards, by hand, to cover the roofs and floors. Many were to work clearing the land, and others used to handling the broad axe, were to hew timbers. Shingles also had to be made by hand and other men were to do the necessary carpenter work in erecting the log houses. Working with this plan, it was felt that two houses with stone chimneys could be erected every day and that in six weeks enough could be built to shelter five hundred people. When the plan was at its height, as many as one hundred and eighty of the refugees were building and clearing land in various settlements. Apparently everyone was able to be housed before the bad weather set in, although the log cabins were often drafty and some let in as much bad weather as they kept out.

Late in 1815 or in early 1816, there were 838 refugees residing in Preston and its vicinity, 44 at Porter's Lake, 131 on Poett's Route, 113 on the Frog Lake Route, 190 on Gardiner's Route, 36 on the Partridge River Route, 139 on the Cole Harbour Route, 46 on Crane's Route, 45 on Bundy's Route, 94 on the road between Lake Loon and the Dartmouth Ferry House, 293 at Hammonds Plains, 80 at Refugee Hill and at the head of the North West Arm, and 59 on the Windsor and Colchester roads. In the communities reported upon, there was a total of 1,316 Black refugees.

In August 1817 Lord Dalhousie, the Lieutenant-Governor of Nova Scotia, reported on a visit he had made to the Black settlements: 'I find almost every man had one or more acres cleared and ready for seed and working with an industry which astonished me.' Dalhousie provided the refugees with 1,500 bushels of seed potatoes as well as cabbages and turnip seeds, 'in proportion to each mans [sic] cleared land', and some nets for fishing and sought a market for the boards and shingles some of them had produced. In a note of caution, however, he advised the Colonial office that rations would have to be issued the following winter and until they could produce sufficient crops 'to feed their numerous families — without it they may perish.'

Years of Hardship

The plan for settling the refugees was successful insofar as it got everyone under a roof. The potential success of the settlements was another question. Many factors worked against it. The settlers had but recently escaped slavery, a system which must have sapped the initiative and drive from people. They also had been used to a hot climate and to plantation crops, neither of which was found in Nova Scotia. Then, too, little of the land on the Atlantic seaboard of Nova Scotia had great agricultural potential and the sections received by the refugees were certainly no better than the average. There can be little doubt that by producing wooden products they were using the land to its best advantage.

Unfortunately, too, they arrived during a particularly cold period. Province-wide crop failures in 1816, the 'year with no summer', and 1817, the 'year of the mice', discouraged even the farmers who had settled on good land, and forced the Black settlers to accept additional government assistance.

The refugees also suffered from colds, influenza, pneumonia and other diseases in the unfamiliar climate in Nova Scotia.

Added to these considerations is the fact that the Black settlers who were dissatisfied with farming could not leave and move on to the United States or elsewhere, as did so many of the other settlers. The Black population could not go back to the United States because they feared a return to slavery. Although some went to the West Indies, completely unfounded rumours of their being sold into slavery there cut off that area as well. For practical considerations it seemed that they had to stay, even if it was not economically advantageous to do so.

Taking all the circumstances into account, coupled with the human problem of racial discrimination, it is perhaps remarkable that they accomplished what they did.

Emigration to Trinidad

Numbers of the Loyalists and many of the later White settlers of Nova Scotia moved on to the United States or to Upper Canada. So, too, did a few of the refugees of the War of 1812. Between the time of their arrival and 1820, some had expressed their desire to start afresh somewhere else. Accordingly, Lieutenant-Governor Sir James Kempt instructed Richard Inglis to visit the Black communities to see how many people wanted to emigrate and offer them an opportunity to go to Trinidad. On August 20, 1820, Inglis reported that he had visited the settlements and that a total of 34 families from Beech Hill (Beechville), Preston, and Hammonds Plains had expressed interest in the plan.

With this assurance, tenders were called for transportation of the refugees to their new home. On January 6, 1821, '81 black men [and women] and 14 children sailed' to Trinidad. On April 17, 1821, Kempt reported that he had received word from Sir Ralph Woodford, the Governor of Trinidad, that the refugees had arrived safely.

The Passing Years

After the Trinidad emigration, the life of the Black settlers of Nova Scotia settled into the day-to-day struggle for existence. Some, like Jeremiah Gardner and like Jacob Allen, who had a wife, a mother-in-law and an apprentice to support, petitioned for and received additional grants of land. Some became moderately successful farmers selling their produce, manufactured goods and wood in the markets of Halifax and other urban centres. Others earned their living by pursuing a trade, either one they possessed before coming to Nova Scotia or one they had acquired after arriving. Some at Hammonds Plains and in the Annapolis Valley became coopers, making barrels for apples and fish and for holding water on board ships. Tradition maintains that the Hammonds Plains people found a steady market in supplying barrels for the Navy in Halifax.

At least one person, a Mr. Campbell, became a successful businessman. In the 1830's it was reported that he owed the chief livery stable in Halifax and his farm and stock compared most favourably with those belonging to Lieutenant-Governor Sir James Kempt. Newspaper records indicate that some became sailors and followed the sea. Others likely learned sailmaking and the various trades associated with the province's 'Golden Age of Sail'. Many of the Blacks, however, remained as unskilled labourers, travelling through the province in the summer seeking work on the farms, and returning to their homes in the fall to live off the charity of their Black neighbours. This practice proved harmful to the entire community, especially during the years when crops were poor. It necessitated government assistance year after year to purchase food and to distribute seed for the coming season.

Together with their White neighbours, the Black settlers had to fight the soil for a living, withstand the ravages of diseases such as smallpox and scarlet fever, and stand counted as part of the Militia forces. However, the Black Militiamen were organized into segregated units of Pioneers, limiting their service to that of labourers. This type of military segregation existed well into the 20th century.

Confirmation of Land Grants

In the mid-1830's, the Nova Scotia House of Assembly received a petition signed by 64 Blacks from Preston, They complained that they had not received the grants of the land they had occupied since 1815-16. At that time, they had understood that after three years of holding a lot of land under a ticket of location, it would be granted to them. This state of affairs often caused great inconvenience, as it was difficult to sell the land without a complete title. Furthermore, as they would not likely be listed as property owners, it would be necessary for them to take the oath of affirmation (by which one swears that he has the right to vote) before they could vote in an election. While the settlers of Hammonds Plains had their grants confirmed in 1836, it was not until May 3, 1842 that the general grant, covering about 1800 acres, to the Black settlers in Preston, was issued.

A Plan for Relocation

In 1837, the House of Assembly noted that the Blacks were not doing well on the land they had received. The House suggested that it might be to the advantage of the Black citizens to be relocated in other parts of the province where the land was richer. The Surveyor-General found land in Pictou and Sydney (Antigonish) Counties which would support the groups from Preston, Hammonds Plains and Beech Hill (Beechville) and he informed the Lieutenant-Governor accordingly. Lieutenant-Governor Sir Colin Campbell then wrote Lord Glenelg, the Secretary of State for the Colonies, and requested permission to carry out the plan if enough of the Black people were interested in it. Glenelg replied, raising a number of objections. He said, first, that after the changes in the Crown Land Act in 1827 and 1831, land was no longer granted, but sold; and, second, he did not wish to set a precedent by relaxing the rules, unless he was sure that the plan would work. As the Government of neither Great Britain nor Nova Scotia was willing to cover the expenses which would accompany such a plan, it was soon forgotten. Not even the labours of Joseph Howe, in whose constituency many of the Blacks lived, could revive the scheme.

Howe described the position of the Black settlers in the province when he wrote:

> *In Nova Scotia, though persons of all complexions are entitled to the same Civil Rights, yet there, as in most other countries, with respect to intermarriage and society, there is a separation between Whites and Blacks.*

Later Emigrations and Immigrations

As the thirties melted into the forties and fifties, Nova Scotia emerged from the prolonged post-war depression and entered what was to be remembered as her 'Golden Age'. Probably the Black Nova Scotians shared the favourable economic climate of the age of sail and booming gold camps. They, too, likely rejoiced at the winning of responsible government in 1848 and split their votes over the question of the Confederation scheme of 1867. But even during the years of prosperity, and in increased numbers in later years, thousands of Nova Scotians, both Black and White, were forced to quit their native province. They went to the industrial centers of New England, to the American mid-west, and to the central and western Canadian provinces seeking employment, for there was none available at home.

In the years preceding the American Civil War and the subsequent freeing of the Amer-

> The "Stag Hotel" is kept by William Dear,
> Outside, the House looks somewhat queer,
> Only Look-in, and there's no fear,
> But you'll find Inside, the best of Cheer;
> Brandy, Whiskey, Hop, Spruce, Ginger Beer,
> Clean Beds, and food for Horses here:
> Round about, both far and near,
> Are Streams for Trout, and Woods for Deer,
> To suit the Public taste, 'tis clear,
> Bill Dear will Labour, so will his dearest dear

The rhyming sign of William Deer's Stag Hotel likely cheered many weary travelers with its promise of bed, board, and service. Inns, stage stops, coffee-houses and taverns were important social and commercial establishments in early Nova Scotia.

ican slaves, thousands of Blacks fled north to freedom. Most of the escapees, following the route of the so-called Underground Railroad, arrived in what is now the province of Ontario. A few, like John William Robertson, author of *The Book of the Bible Against Slavery,* arrived in Nova Scotia. Robertson left his master in the southern United States and made his way, with a number of hair-raising escapes, to Boston. From there, he travelled to Halifax, where he found employment and, it is to be hoped, peace. Southern racist feelings were brought home to Maritimers when they read in their papers of Captain Vaughan of Saint John, New Brunswick. While in Savannah, Georgia, he was tarred and feathered by a White mob because 'he had allowed Blacks to eat at his table and had said that a Black man was as good as a White man.'

During the latter part of the nineteenth century, numbers of West Indians immigrated to the province. They usually settled in the urban centers. Many went to the Sydney area seeking employment in the coal mines and steel mills. Another group came from Alabama in 1899 to work at the iron furnace in Sydney.

Today descendants of the Black immigrants in various parts of the province and elsewhere in Canada are making strong contributions to their country, and these are becoming more widely known, but there is a lack of readily available documentation to reveal the full story of the early settlers.

The Stag Hotel, a clever play upon the name of the proprietor, William Deer, was an "Inn" located in Preston, Halifax County, N.S. An example of entrepreneurialism in a Black community, it was sometimes the terminus of Lieutenant-Governor Joseph Howe's carriage drives.

'And The People Said Amen'

During the days of slavery one of the few opportunities for the slaves to congregate was at funerals and other religious services. In their services, and especially their spirituals, they expressed their grievances, and their faith: 'Nobody Knows the Trouble I've Seen', 'Swing Low, Sweet Chariot', and many other hymns told of their unquenchable thirst for freedom, if not in this world, then surely in the next. For many their religion was their great strength and its promise their only hope.

Some of the Blacks who came to Nova Scotia brought the Christian religion with them, while others gained it after they arrived. Black ministers came with their congregations and spread the Gospel throughout the province. The Baptist, David George, was one of the first of the Black religious leaders. He arrived in Halifax by 1785. He preached and converted and baptised both Black and White followers in Shelburne, Birchtown, Halifax, Preston, Saint John, and Fredericton. His work was complemented by that of Boston King and the Methodist Moses Wilkinson and other religious leaders. As remained the case for many years, Black religious leaders were also Black secular leaders. When the Black Loyalists left for Sierra Leone in 1792, many of their ministers went with them. The Blacks who remained in Nova Scotia had their local religious leaders, like Dempsey Jordan in Tracadie, and missionaries from the Roman Catholic and Anglican churches. But they had to wait some years for the arrival of the next great Black religious leader.

Richard Preston arrived in Halifax in 1814, seeking his mother, who had preceded him north. He did not know where she had gone, but was determined to find her. Travelling to Preston, he sought shelter at a house along the way, and the door was opened by his mother, who recognized her long-separated son by a scar on his face. In Halifax he joined the Rev. Mr. (Father) Burton's church and before long his ability as a leader was realized. To prepare for the ministry, he was sent with the support of Rev. Mr. Burton and others to Great Britain, where he studied theology. He returned from England in 1832. In that same year he organized the African Baptist Church on Cornwallis Street in Halifax. During the remaining years of his ministry, Preston organized churches in every county between Halifax and Yarmouth. One of his great triumphs was in 1854 at Granville Mountain where he met with delegates of twelve African Baptist Churches to form the African Baptist Association of Nova Scotia.

Richard Preston was also a leader in the forces favouring the abolition of slavery. He had been in England during the abolition debates which led to the Act of 1833 and had become a familiar figure to Clarkson and Wilberforce and others of the great liberals. Preston himself had been a slave and when he lectured on the subject, in both England and Nova Scotia, he could relate personal experiences. He was President of the Abolitionists in Halifax and was in communication with the abolitionist societies in Boston and other cities. Unfortunately, when he died in 1861, his prayers had not yet been answered, since slavery still existed in the United States and elsewhere at the time of his death.

The Nova Scotia government and several church societies aided in the construction and maintenance of churches in the Black communities. Often, without this support the churches would not have been built or, if built, would have disappeared. Not all the Blacks in Nova Scotia were Baptist. There was also an African Episcopal Methodist Church in Halifax. The early census reports indicate that some of the Black people adhered to the teachings of the Presbyterians and others to the Church of England; and a small number were Roman Catholic. Although the churches were often segregated by the choice of the members, this may have

One of the great leaders of the Black Church in Nova Scotia, Richard Preston was a man of energy, ability and perserverance. McKerrow describes him as being "of ready wit, humorous, and a good extemporaneous speaker," and "as fluent on the platform as in the pulpit."

This sketch of Richard Preston by Dr. J.B. Gilpin was drawn in the 1850s and portrays an intinerant preacher carrying religion to his often widespread and isolated congregation. By carriage or on horseback, Preston traveled from Halifax to Yarmouth preaching and establishing churches.

been unfortunate, as it might have been responsible for setting a pattern of racial segregation throughout society. There is no doubt that whatever their religious affiliation might have been, the churches played a central role in the life of the Black communities in Nova Scotia. Unlike today, when Black leaders represent many professions and positions, in the past the ministry was the major avenue for a capable and ambitous person to gain a position of respect and leadership.

The Role of Education

Obtaining an education in Nova Scotia prior to 1864-65 was often a difficult matter. The creation of a school usually depended on the emphasis that the community placed on the importance of education. If the community felt that education was not important or that it was too costly, then in most cases there would be no school. The Provincial Assembly was willing to support education and every year granted thousands of pounds to aid the local school boards. But there was no real policy regarding assistance, it usually being granted on the petitioned request of the needy school. The Education Acts of 1864-65 created a policy under which education was supported by universal taxation and schools were given regular grants.

With the coming of the Black Loyalists, the real history of Black education begins. In the later 1780s, Colonel Stephen Bluck was the school master in the Black community of Birchtown, near Shelburne. Other schools existed among the Blacks, including those supplied by the Church of England's Society for the Propagation of the Gospel. The Church also supported schools and churches for the use of the Maroons.

Following the arrival of the refugees of the War of 1812, other schools were opened. In 1814, there were 37 Black children attending the Royal Acadian School in Halifax. Sunday and evening schools, in which reading, writing, sewing and navigation were taught, were also sponsored by St. Paul's Anglican Church. Black students could also be found in such schools as the National or Madras system and those supplied by various philanthropic groups. One of these groups, "The Associates of the Late Dr. Bray", by 1830 supported schools for the Black communities in Halifax, Preston, Hammonds Plains, Shelburne and Digby. Often these schools provided the only formal education available to Black children, until early in the twentieth century. In Halifax, there was also the segregated African School supported by government grants. Outside Halifax and the various Black school districts, educational opportunities for Black children depended upon local school authorities.

By Nova Scotia law, the school commissioners of any municipality could, with government approval, establish separate schools, if they considered them necessary. Few such schools were established under this law, because residential separation was the most common cause of segregated schools. However, three separate schools were established in Halifax. Many Blacks were content with this arrangement and desired to have these schools maintained for them. Others did not, and in 1884 the House of Assembly received two petitions against the separate schools.

In the full debate that resulted, some supported the status quo and others condemned it. Some members sought to have any reference to colour struck from the Education Act. It has been stated that those who desired this end had the best of the argument and the worst of the vote — at any rate, they did not succeed in abolishing the separate schools. The Bill on Education passed in 1884 continued to permit the Government to establish schools for different sexes and colours. However, Black pupils could not be excluded from instruction in the district in which they lived, and if no Black school existed, they were supposed to be guaranteed by law admission to the public school. The Education Act of 1918 continued to allow the establishment of separate schools and so the law remained until 1954, when all reference to race was removed from the statute.

During these years, students, both Black and White, suffered perhaps not so much from having separate schools as from having no schools at all. The continued high expense associated with education often made it impossible for the local districts to pay a teacher a competitive salary or to maintain the school buildings. The School Inspector's Reports often commented on the schools that had been closed for years and the need for even itinerant teachers and for more money. Today an improving education system is better supplying the needs of the people. And it is in education, not only in the scholastic sense, but in the broad area of human development, that the hope for the future lies.

Black Nova Scotians to 1901

In the decades between 1861 and 1901 Black Nova Scotians experienced only a limited increase in numbers. In 1861 there were 5,927 Blacks reported among the province's total population of 330,857, or 1.8 percent. In 1871, by which time Nova Scotia had become a part of the new Dominion of Canada, the Black population had reached 6,212 but was only 1.6 percent of the provincial population. This figure represented 29 percent of the 21,496 Blacks recorded among Canada's 3,689,257 citizens. Ten years later the 1881 census listed 7,062 Blacks among the 440,572 people in Nova Scotia. That same year the population of Canada was 4,434,810.

The years between 1881 and 1901 were not good ones for Nova Scotians generally. In those twenty years the population of the province increased only by a little more than 19,000 people to 459,574. During those same twenty years, the reported Black population of Nova Scotia actually showed a decrease of 1,078 persons, with only 5,984 recorded in 1901 — the lowest Black population total for thirty years. The 1901 census also reported a total of only 17,437 Blacks in all of Canada. This figure was also a thirty year low so it may well be that both the Nova Scotian and Canadian figures were not completely accurate. Whether correct or not, the figures show more than just a stagnant population in the province. These figures also indicated the economic conditions that prevailed in Nova Scotia, which affected all residents of the province.

An economic depression hit Canada in the fall of 1873 and remained until the later years of the 1890s. While the discovery of gold in the Klondike and the opening of the Canadian west brought renewed prosperity to much of Canada, times remained hard in the Maritimes. These adverse economic conditions caused a general lack of opportunity which forced hundreds of people out of work and caused widespread hardship. It is likely that this was particularly hard on the Black workers, who, in the best of times, were often the last hired and the first let go. During these depression years thousands of Nova Scotians left their native province and went to "Upper Canada" or to the "Boston states" looking for work. Some eventually returned. Many more did not, and a good percentage of the Black populations of Toronto, Montreal and other cities can trace their roots to Nova Scotian ancestors.

As 1899 became 1900 the Prime Minister of Canada, Sir Wilfred Laurier, confidently proclaimed that "the twentieth century belongs to Canada". The turn of the century was not, however, a good time for Blacks in Nova Scotia or in Canada as a whole. Throughout the country the Black population was largely ignored by politicians and victimized by discrimination, while educators overlooked the existence of Black history.

The story of the Black Nova Scotians is an on-going one, a story of many chapters and parts, without which the history of Nova Scotia and Canada is incomplete. The story is one of failures and successes; it is the history of a people — a history that must be remembered, and a story that must be told.

A Part of the Life

Black Nova Scotians have contributed to the development of Nova Scotia. Along with Nova Scotians of other racial origins, they have participated in the struggle for self-improvement and a better life, a struggle which provides the impetus for the growth of the entire province. Thousands of Blacks have lived and died in Nova Scotia, as have many other Nova Scotians, with little public recognition of their contribution, but this does not make their contribution any less important. A few Blacks have become known for their extraordinary achievements and have, through their work, given a profound demonstration of the significance of their race to the total fabric of this province's rich heritage — a heritage which includes many people of different colours, creeds, races, religions, national backgrounds, and ethnic origins. Following are brief descriptions of some of the Black Nova Scotians who have distinguished themselves in various ways.

George Dixon
1870-1909

Known as "Little Chocolate" to fight fanciers, Dixon was born in Halifax, Nova Scotia, on July 29, 1870. He moved to Boston when he was very young. He had a natural love for the boxing game and soon developed into one of the best amateurs for his weight in the Boston area. He became so good that when he was nineteen years old and weighed 112 pounds, he won over Eugene Horabacher, then the reigning sensation in his weight-class, in two rounds. Dixon soon became a great drawing card. This Canadian Black was the first boxer to win three world titles: paperweight, bantamweight and featherweight championships at different times. Dixon held the featherweight title longer than anyone, with the exception of Johnny Kilbane. Ten years as undisputed champion, however, gave Dixon a complacent attitude. He was below peak condition when he was stopped by Terrible Terry McGovern in New York in January, 1900. Dixon kept on fighting until his health gave way. He died in 1909, a boxer never to be forgotten. The George Dixon Drop-in Centre and Playground on Gottingen Street in Halifax commemorates this well-known fighter.

Dr. William Harvey Goler
1846-1939

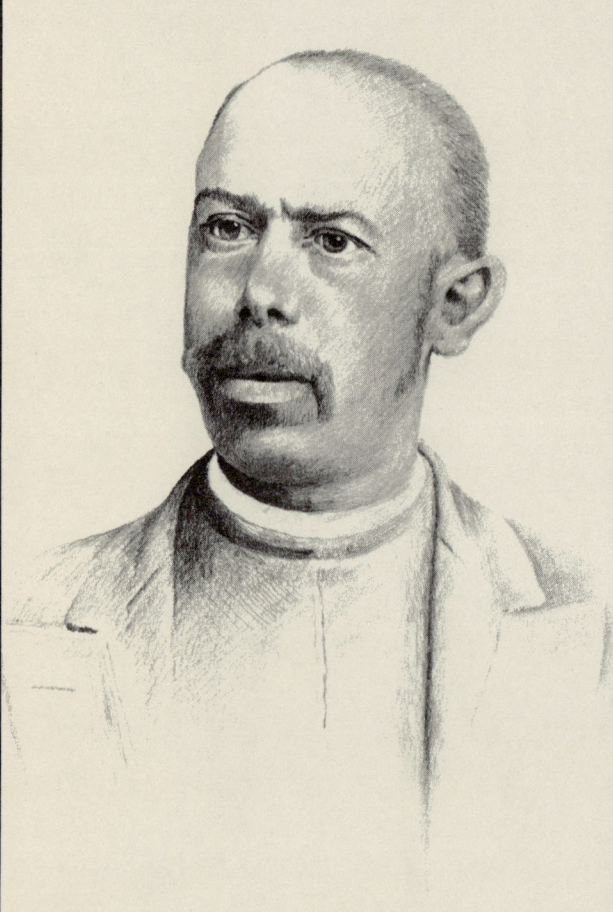

William Harvey Goler, the only Black Nova Scotian known to have become president of a college, was born in Halifax on January 1, 1846, son of Harvey and Katherine Goler. His parents died when he was young and at the age of 15 he was apprenticed to the firm of Coleman and Brown, bricklayers and plasterers, of Halifax. After he finished his apprenticeship, Goler moved to Boston where wages were higher. He worked at his trade until 1873 when he entered Lincoln University in Pennsylvania. Valedictorian of the class of '78, he went on to receive a degree in theology. His first appointment was pastor of St. Matthew's Methodist Episcopal Church in Greensboro, North Carolina. Later he accepted an appointment to head the history and philosophy department of Livingstone College in Salisbury, North Carolina, then known as Zion Wesley Institute. He also served as industrial superintendent, an administrative post that was sorely needed to aid the struggling institution to survive financially. As a result of his services, he received from Lincoln University, at the age of 45, the honourary degree of Doctor of Divinity. Three years later, Dr. Goler was made president of Livingstone College, a position he held until 1916. During his stay in office, he came to the relief of the institution's straitened circumstances more than once with his own private funds. After resignation, he became financial secretary of the African Methodist Episcopal Zion Church. In this capacity, Dr. Goler served until 1932, when he retired because of poor health. Livingstone, which now has roughly 700 students, has inherited the bulk of his fortune which he derived mainly through investments in real estate.

William Edward Hall, VC
1826-1904

Hall was the son of a Black slave from Virginia who sought sanctuary in Nova Scotia during the War of 1812. Although there is some uncertainty about his actual birthdate, Hall was born in the vicinity of Horton Bluff. He went to sea as boy and joined the Royal Navy in 1852 as an able seaman aboard HMS *Rodney*. He served with distinction during the Crimean War. In 1857 he was serving aboard HMS *Shannon* during the Indian Mutiny. He volunteered to go with a naval gun brigade to relieve Lucknow. The brigade members dragged the ship's guns over rough countryside until they were outside the walls of the besieged city. Heavy fire rendered one gun and its crew out of action; only Hall and a badly-wounded officer were left with the other gun. Hall kept the gun firing and one of his shots breached the wall sufficiently to enable the relieving forces to push through to join the defenders. For his courage and devotion to duty, Queen Victoria awarded the Victoria Cross, the most highly prized of all medals, to Hall. He was the first Canadian to be so honoured. A branch of the Royal Canadian Legion in Halifax bears his name.

B. A. Husbands
?-1968

Best known as "the smiling president of the Halifax Coloured Citizens Improvement League," B. A. Husbands spent his time and money on the betterment of children, both black and white, for more than thirty years. He organized the League and served as president from 1932. Mr. Husbands was first employed by H. R. Silver, prominent Halifax merchant. In 1957, he retired from HMC dockyard. His distinguished services in the Second World War earned him the Order of the British Empire, conferred on him by King George VI. He also received a coronation medal in recognition of his work in welcoming and entertaining Navy personnel. During the war years the League arranged entertainment for thousands of servicemen in Halifax. B. A. Husbands received letters of appreciation from many prominent people, including Ramsay MacDonald (former British Prime Minister), Franklin D. Roosevelt and Mrs. Roosevelt, Sir Winston Churchill, John F. Kennedy, and Pope John XXIII. Leader in the civil rights movement for many years, Mr. Husbands' efforts broke the colour bar prohibiting Black women as student nurses in Halifax training hospitals, and he led the fight for equality in educational and vocational opportunities for Nova Scotia Blacks. B. A. Husbands died in Halifax, June 20, 1968.

Sam Langford
1884-1956

Sam Langford, the Boston Tar Baby, was considered by many to have been one of the greatest fighters in the history of boxing. Langford was born in Weymouth, Nova Scotia, and when he was 14 years old, he left home and went to Boston to seek work. He got a job cleaning a small fight club run by Joe Woodman. Woodman became his manager and trained the young fighter. Between 1902 and 1923, Langford fought some 642 bouts. Although he was five foot, six inches in height and his top weight was 162½ pounds, he fought many heavyweight fighters and defeated most of them. Sam Langford travelled around the world as uncrowned heavyweight champion, but was unable to get a title bout. In 1917 he lost the sight of his right eye. Woodman urged him to give up boxing, but Langford refused to quit. He fought for seven more years until, in 1924, he became totally blind. Sam Langford fought at a time when Black fighters battled not only their ring opponents, but prejudice as well, and he made a great contribution to the role of his race in the competitive sports world. His memory is kept alive in his home area today by the "Sam Langford Community Centre" at Weymouth Falls.

Portia White
1910-1968

Portia White was born in Truro, daughter of Dr. W. A. White. She made her musical debut at the age of six in her father's church choir. At seventeen, Miss White was teaching school and taking singing lessons. When she won a silver cup at the Nova Scotia Music Festival, the Halifax Ladies' Musical Club granted her a scholarship to the Halifax Conservatory of Music. This gave her the first big boost. She made a successful debut in Toronto in 1941, followed by other concert appearances. In 1944 she made her New York debut and subsequently toured the United States, Canada, and Europe. Early in her career, the Nova Scotia Government set up a fund to help Miss White receive top vocal training. Known as the Nova Scotia Talent Trust, this fund is still in operation providing financial assistance to many outstanding young performers of our province. A highlight in Miss White's career was singing before Queen Elizabeth at the opening of Confederation Centre in Charlottetown in 1964. Portia White died in Toronto in 1968. In September of the following year, the Halifax City Regional Library Board received a $1,000 gift from her estate to assist in the purchase of books and materials on music. This is a valuable asset to the cultural development of the Halifax region, and serves as a living memorial of Portia White's affection for both music and her native province.

Dr. William A. White
1874-1936

Dr. White was born in Virginia in 1874, the son of slaves. He went to school in Baltimore and in 1898 he came to Nova Scotia to study divinity at Acadia University. During his years there, Dr. White was a star in track and field and rugby. After graduating from Acadia in 1903, he performed missionary work for about a year around Nova Scotia. During this period, Dr. White founded the New Glasgow Second Baptist Church. Then he had a call to Truro, where he preached from 1905 to 1915. In March of 1916, Dr. White went overseas with the Second Construction Battalion as the only Black chaplain in the British Empire. While overseas, he was called to Cornwallis Street Baptist Church in Halifax where he remained until his death. Dr. White was the first Black minister to preach at the Baptist Convention in Wolfville. One of his outstanding achievements was the monthly broadcast to Canada and parts of the United States of his services from Cornwallis Street Baptist Church. In June of 1936, his *alma mater* honoured him with a doctoral degree. That September he died after a lifetime of devotion and courage.

Bibliography

ARCHIBALD, ADAMS. "Story of the Deportation of Negroes from Nova Scotia to Sierra Leone". *Nova Scotia Historical Society Collections,* v.7, 1891, pp.129-154.

BEST, CARRIE. *That Lonesome Road: The Autobiography of Carrie M. Best.* New Glasgow, Clarion, 1977

BLAKELEY, PHYLLIS R. "Boston King: A Negro Loyalist in Nova Scotia". *Dalhousie Review,* v. 48, 1968, pp. 347-357.

_____ "William Hall, Canada's First Naval V.C." *Dalhousie Review,* v. 37, 1957, pp. 250-258.

BYMNER, DOUGLAS, "The Jamaica Maroons — How They Came to Nova Scotia — How They Left It". *Royal Society of Canada Proceedings and Transactions,* Series 2, v. 1, 1895, pp. 81-90.

CLAIRMONT, DONALD H. and DENNIS W. MAGILL. *Africville: The Life and Death of a Canadian Black Community.* Toronto, McClelland and Stewart, 1974.

FERGUSSON, C. BRUCE. *A Documentary Study of the Establishment of the Negroes in Nova Scotia Between the War of 1812 and the Winning of Responsible Government.* The Public Archives of Nova Scotia, Publication No. 8, 1948.

FYFE, C. "Thomas Peters: History and Legend". *Sierra Leone Studies,* New Series, v. 1, 1953, pp. 4-13.

HENRY, FRANCES. *Forgotten Canadians: The Blacks of Nova Scotia.* Canadian Social Problems Series. Don Mills, Ontario, Longman (Canada), 1973.

MACKERROW, P.E. *A Brief History of the Colored Baptists of Nova Scotia.* Halifax,

N.S., Nova Scotia Printing Company, 1895. Reprinted by Afro Nova Scotian Enterprises, (Halifax, N.S.) 1976 and introduced, edited, footnoted & annotated by Frank S. Boyd, Jr.

PACHI, BRIDGLAL. *Canadian Black Studies.* St. Mary's University, Halifax, N.S., International Education Centre, 1979.

SMITH, T. W. "The Slave in Canada". *Nova Scotia Historical Society Collections,* v. 10, 1899, pp. 3-161.

SPRAY, W. A. *The Blacks in New Brunswick.* Fredericton, Brunswick Press, 1972.

WALKER, JAMES W. *The Black Loyalists.* N.Y., Africana Publishing Co., 1976.

WALKER, JAMES. W. *Black Canadian History: A Study Guide for Teachers and Students.* Department of the Secretary of State, 1979.

WALKER, JAMES W. *Identity: The Black Experience in Canada.* Toronto, Gage, 1979.

WINKS, ROBIN W. *The Blacks in Canada: A History.* New Haven, Yale University Press, 1971.